A Guide to Historic
Haworth and the Brontës

by
Mark Ward
with
Ann Dinsdale and Robert Swindells

Foreword by
Robert Swindells

Hendon Publishing Company

First edition 2000
by
Mulberry Books
Second impression 2007
by
Hendon Publishing Company
© **Mark Ward 2000, 2007**

Cover photograph by
Simon Warner

Cover design by
Anthony Finnerty

Photographs by
Simon Warner
(except where indicated)

Illustrated by
Sophie Greenwood

Layout and typesetting
Barbara Gordon

ISBN 978086067 1602
Printed by
Fretwell Print and Design
for Hendon Publishing Company, Hendon Mill
Nelson, Lancashire, BB9 8AD

The Authors

Mark Ward has presented an Alaskan radio show, built film sets in Africa and worked for a New Zealand production company. For a number of years he was Haworth's official tour guide. Publications include: *Life in many Living rooms*, (Alaskan Small Press, 1993) *The Dark Unquiet Hills,* Mullberry Books, 1995) and *Used Rhymes,* (Ausstieher, 2007)

Ann Dinsdale has lived most of her life in West Yorkshire. She is Collections Manager at the Brontë Parsonage Museum at Haworth, where she is involved with organising exhibitions and caring for the collections. She lectures and writes on aspects of the Brontës' lives and social conditions in mid-nineteenth century Haworth. She is the author of *Old Haworth*, (Hendon Publishing,1999) *The Brontës at Haworth* (Francis Lincon, 2006), *The Brontë Connection* (Hendon Publishing, 2007).

Robert Swindells is a native of Bradford who has lived in Haworth for the last 21 years. He has been a proof reader, airman, engineering inspector, clerk, security guard, shop assistant, bingo checker, barman and teacher. Since 1980 he has made his living writing fiction for young people. His novel *A Wish For Wings*, was inspired by his discovery of the Amy Johnson stone featured in Walk Four in this publication.) The stone has since been stolen.

Contents

Foreword

This book is both highly informative and immensely entertaining. Besides a history and pre-history of Haworth and biographical details about its most celebrated family, the reader is regaled with accounts of murders, unexplained disappearances, a gold rush, a whip-wielding cleric, an overcrowded graveyard, a bizarre parachute accident and other quirky proofs of the fact that Haworth was never a sleepy little spot where nothing happens.

The four walks herein described with meticulous clarity have been designed to lead the walker close to the sites of some of the bizarre, often tragic events mentioned above, as well as to afford some spectacular views of the wild hill country from which the Brontë sisters and their unjustly maligned brother drew inspiration.

Read the stories. Walk the walks. You'll be fitter, happier and hungrier as a result. In a village full of eateries, who could ask for more?

Robert Swindells

Dedicated to my friends,
the villagers of Haworth, Stanbury and
Oxenhope.

Acknowledgements

Special thanks to the following:
Bob and Brenda Swindells, the staff of Haworth
Tourist Information Centre - past and present,
The Brontë Parsonage Museum, Joanne Walker,
Chris and Jon at Nettcom Solutions Limited and
Albert Smart.

Haworth and the Moors

A Brief History

Evidence of human habitation of the area dates back some eight thousand years to when Stone Age hunter-gatherers migrated north to the region tracking the elk, wild horses and boar through the great forest which covered the area. In the mineral rich soils left by the receding ice sheet some two thousand years earlier, an abundance of flora and fauna flourished whilst large streams, now generally insignificant due to the building of reservoirs, teemed with a variety of fish. With such a ready food supply man slowly began clearing the trees on the high ground and settling the area. With the advent of agriculture to the region, between five and six thousand years ago, in the form of domestication of crops and livestock, forest gave way to cultivation and the landscape that we see today began to take shape.

By 500BC the trees had all but disappeared on the high ground and man began to settle in the lower regions. The remains of three thousand year old settlements in the form of Bronze Age earthworks can still be found on the surrounding hills. For the next two-thousand years Haworth's history becomes enveloped in a mist as thick and impenetrable as any which regularly enfolds its hills and valleys.

Apart from its name, a derivative of the Norse/ Saxon Ha and Worth, meaning an enclosed piece of land or farmstead, we have no recorded evidence of Haworth until the Domesday survey of 1086 which lists seven berwicks or villages coming under the jurisdiction of the Manor of Bradford. These included Haworth, Stanbury and Oxenhope. The Manor was in the possession of a Saxon Earl named Gamel who had managed to retain some of his ancestral lands post 1066, probably through swearing allegiance to the Conqueror.

Kirkbey's inquest of 1296 holds that one Godfrey de Haworth held four oxgangs in the area, whilst extracts from the Archbishop's registers and wills of York from 1300 all show the antiquity and comparative importance of

Haworth Church. In 1317 a decree was issued commanding the rector and vicar of Bradford and the freeholders of Haworth to pay the curate of Haworth Chapel the salary due to him for which they had been liable from ancient times.

However, it isn't until the poll tax survey of 1381 that we can get any idea of population size. The survey lists forty people as inhabitants of Haworth, each paying 4d. The tax was levied according to income with 4d being the basic rate for those aged over sixteen, whereas merchants, landowners etc. paid more. Married couples were charged at a single rate whilst mendicants, serfs and the infirm paid nothing. From this we can estimate Haworth's population to be around two hundred people.

From the sixteenth-century onwards small farms began appearing on the landscape and the dual industries of wool production and weaving flourished in the area. Land, which the removal of tree cover had turned to wind swept moorland, was enclosed and cultivated, and the remains of some of these farms are still visible today, a testament to the men and women who attempted to eke out a living from land which the moor was constantly trying to reclaim.

Stone replaced wood and turf as the main building material. Quarries were opened to supply the demand, cutting into the hills surrounding the village. The colonisation of the moor occurred at such a rapid rate that Daniel Defoe was to comment in 1725 that the moor resembled a continuous village.

By the mid eighteenth-century England was still an agricultural society. However, both social and industrial change was quickening the agricultural revolution, and land enclosure acts which took away what common grazing land remained were forcing people into the towns and villages. By the end of the century water-powered mills had begun to appear in the Worth Valley, later to be replaced by steam. Small mining companies were set up, eager to exploit the coal seams, the extracted coal stoking the boilers in the local factories. The industrial revolution had arrived. It was the beginning of the end for the cottage industries which had flourished successfully for two hundred years. Halliwell Sutcliffe, the local novelist, lamented the arrival of steam:

"Steam, it seems to me, has done more to degrade man than any other discovery the world has known, it has substituted hurry for patience, and

greed for the old quiet wish to earn as much as mind and body needed for ordinary comfort. It has drawn men to the towns, and the towns have always been a sort of cancerous growth, and it has substituted the hideous conditions of the factory for the same healthy handiwork that was done in country cottages."

Haworth Churchyard with its mass of graves bears silent witness to the hardships of nineteenth-century life. It was into this changing environment that Patrick Brontë arrived with his family to take up the position of perpetual curate of Haworth parish in 1820.

Walk One

Penistone Hill via Sowdens Farm

*Distance: approximately 1¹/₂ miles
circular route*

Once a thriving mining and quarrying community, Penistone Hill provided a vital source of employment to the people of Haworth throughout the industrial age. Now the area is a designated country park, its saws and hammers long since silenced and its buildings removed, giving way instead to a wide variety of plant and animal species. However, upon closer inspection, and with a little imagination, one can still find evidence of these workings at what would have been a noisy, bustling place, where shafts were sunk and tunnels dug extracting coal to feed the furnaces of the local steam powered factories, and quarries were hewn into the hillside providing stone for the rapidly expanding village and surrounding towns.

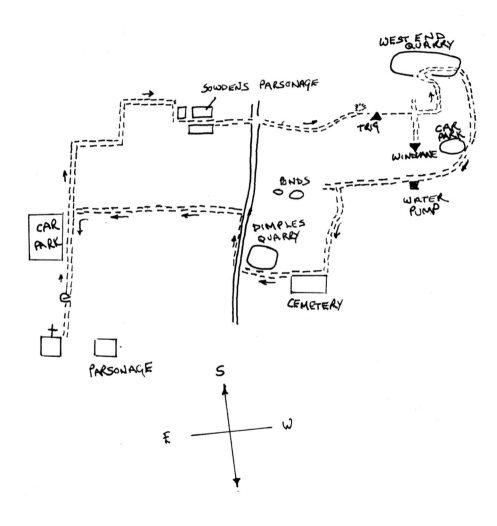

Leave Haworth churchyard through the south facing iron kissing-gate and continue along the path following the sign for the Brontë Way/Oxenhope.

After passing through a small wooden gate, keep the wall to your right and continue up the path to the farm directly facing, go through the gate and to the right of the house bringing you into the farmyard itself.

Mark E Ward

Sowdens Farm

The old Haworth Parsonage, pre 1779

The stone porch is all that remains of an earlier house originally built in the early 1600s.

Extensive building alterations through the eighteenth and nineteenth centuries have changed the remainder of the house considerably. Between the years 1742-1763 it was the home of the Revd. William Grimshaw, a man held in such high regard that Patrick Brontë deemed it a great honour to have been given the parish of such an esteemed predecessor.

The Evangelical Revival

During the mid eighteenth-century people were becoming disillusioned with the church. Many self-ordained preachers were taking to the road spreading various forms of the gospel throughout the country. The church came to regard these soapbox preachers as a nuisance at best, and at worst, very dangerous.

The established church was beginning to rock as unrest began to set in. The evangelical revival movement came about as a means of trying to refocus the general populace into what the church believed to be their spiritual and physical duty to God.

Three men of note stand out from the many that were involved in this revival: William Grimshaw, John Wesley and George Whitfield.

Mark E Ward

William Grimshaw

For me to live is Christ, to die is gain

Although initially attracted to the church for all the wrong reasons, Grimshaw's moral stance and relentless pursuit of God's cause would in later life not only earn him the respect of the people of Haworth, but would also make him a household name across the country.

If Grimshaw's earlier life within the church had been somewhat misspent, in the pursuit of drinking, gambling and carousing, certain events, most notably the death of his wife, gave him cause to rethink. By the time of his arrival in Haworth in 1742, he was a changed man, going about his business with unerring enthusiasm.

He focussed his attention on what he referred to as the 'heathen practices' of the local inhabitants. These included horse races on the Sabbath, foot races in which the runners would be stripped to the waist, and arvills or funeral feasts which would last for several days, a remnant from the Viking past.

Despite his obvious zealous tendencies, he reputedly visited the pubs prior to his services, driving people out and into the church brandishing a horsewhip. His genuine concern for the people's well-being coupled with his boundless energy (he would walk up to ten miles on winter nights in order to visit the frail and elderly) earned him the admiration and respect of the local inhabitants.

He extended Haworth Church in 1755 (by then his congregation had swelled to over a thousand) and began a subscription fund for the building of the Methodist Chapel on West Lane. He died in 1763 and is buried at Luddenden Foot near Halifax. Part of Grimshaw's three-decker pulpit can be seen in Stanbury Church. (See Walk Two.)

Continue up the farm track in a westerly direction crossing the road and taking the footpath to the right of the telegraph pole following it around and up to the summit.

The large pond as you look down the hill is thought to be the flooded shaft of an early coal mine, near which can be seen a circular path where a horse-gin or hoist, used to extract the coal, may have stood.

Continue along the top of the hill heading towards the white Ordnance Survey triangulation point.

The large hole on your left just prior to the TRIG point was one of the numerous air shafts servicing the network of tunnels deep beneath the hillside, where children sometimes as young as ten years old were used to take the coal from the coal face to the hoist.

Carry on along the path, turning right at the crossroads, where you'll come to a large stone slab.

The markings on the stone indicate where a windvane once stood. The vane was connected by cable and chains to a pumping station, visible directly below in a small cleft at the base of the hill. Water was pumped out of the mines and over the hill, where it was used to cool the steam powered stone saws in the quarry behind. Each day the vane had to be manually turned into the prevailing wind, and one day a quarryman tragically died when his clothing became entangled in the chain. The mine itself, now capped, is the circular area of grey shale to the left of the pumping station.

Now, turning back on yourself, walk along the path in a south-easterly direction towards the distant windmills on Ovenden Moor. At the crossroads turn right following a well-marked track in a westerly direction for a short distance before turning left and continuing to the edge of the quarry.

On the site of what is now the car park, facing, stood a number of buildings erected to service the quarry, the raised triangular stone marks the location of the blacksmith's forge, where tools for the quarry were made and repaired.

Take the footpath which should be directly in front of you, down into the quarry itself. It is rather steep, and those who can't manage it should follow the path around to the west, coming into the quarry from that direction. In the base of the quarry turn right, walking towards the orange sandstone rockface.

Current or Cross Bedding

West End Quarry

Formed in running water, the banks of sand were pushed up and moved along by the river. As the tops of the migrating sandbanks were eroded by the current, new sand banks would build up on them, and sometimes sand sank into softer mud below, creating a trough-like effect in the rock face. Local quarrymen would rarely use cross-bedded sandstone as it couldn't be trimmed off squarely. Large slabs of this discarded sandstone can be found around the hillside, many of them bearing the marks of the plugs and 'feathers' used to split the stone. A series of holes would be drilled, into each of which would be placed two 'feathers' (like small metal shoe horns), a steel plug would then be driven between them

Mark E Ward

causing the stone to split evenly. The hole in the rock face is known as a 'mare'. These are natural formations found in sandstone, in which the composition differs from the surrounding rock. Soft and rich in iron, it was known locally as 'donkey stone', and was in the past used to clean and polish stone steps.

Continue out of the quarry in a westerly direction, following a small cleft in the hillside to your right, bringing you around into Moorside Quarry car park. From there take the path to the right running along the base of the hill, heading back towards Haworth.

The area of grassland at the back of the quarry is known as Penistone Slack. This was the site of a horse fair which took place annually in the nineteenth-century.

Carry along passing the water pump to your left for approximately thirty metres, then take the path to your left following until you come to the edge of Haworth Cemetery. Turn right along the path running parallel to the wall and continue along until it brings you down into Dimples Quarry.

Ancient Sea Beds

Millions of years ago the north of England was covered by sea. Huge rivers poured into the delta from the north and east, carrying with them the sediments and sand worn from ancient rock. These would eventually build up and compress to form the millstone grit prevalent in this area. The continuation of this process over time eventually silted up the delta forcing the sea out. With the sea no longer covering, and the ground rich in minerals, plant life began to flourish creating swamps and forests of large seed bearing pine. Throughout this period sea levels were constantly rising and falling and would periodically drown the forest enabling the whole sedimentary process to begin again. Today we find our coal seams sandwiched between these soft and hard layers of rock.

At the end of the upper carboniferous period some 280 million years ago, massive earth movements forced up the Pennines whilst at the same time pushing out the sea. Dramatic climatic changes occurred, creating a dry arid desert. Over the next 278 million years, wind and sand ground away at the Pennine ridge, eventually flattening them out and allowing the sea to encroach once more, until earth movements forced the Pennines up once again giving us what we have today. The reason why the major coal deposits are situated either side of the Pennines is due to this initial erosion.

The face at Dimples Quarry is unique in that it gives us a very clear picture of how this whole rock forming process actually occurred, building up at the rate of $1/4$ inch (6mm) every sixty-three years. We can count the ridges as we would the rings on a tree. The various sandwiched layers run from top to bottom as follows:

- Orange delta sandstone.

- Silts and shales containing small plant fragments and ripple marks (shale being compressed marine mud).

- Thin coal seam - which eventually thickens out into the extensive coal fields of Yorkshire, Derbyshire and Nottinghamshire.

- White plant soil.

- Grey coastal sandstone.

- Delta sandstone.

Walking around the small pond and up to the rock face itself, approximately at eye level,

Mark E Ward

you'll see the fossilized branch from one of the large pine trees which covered the area millions of years ago.

Man has always been adept at using his environment, and the shale was used in the making of bricks. Moss from the ponds was used as an absorbent for dressing wounds whilst the peat, which turns water the colour of cold tea, was used as a dye in the making of brown paper.

Come out of the quarry onto Dimples Lane turning right then first left. At the bottom of the track turn left again. The path will bring you back to Haworth Church.

Walk Two

Top Withens ('Wuthering Heights')

Distance: approximately 7 miles circular route

Walk up Church Street by the side of the King's Arms, past the Church and Parsonage, following the footpath along the back of the houses and on through the field. Go through the gate onto West Lane and turn left, then left again onto Cemetery Road, continuing along for approximately 150 metres until you come to the gates of the 'new' Haworth cemetery, opened at the end of the nineteenth-century, as a result of the old churchyard being grossly overcrowded. Walk through the kissing gate and up the tree-lined path to the gates of the cemetery itself. Just to your right on the front row facing stands the black granite monument to Lily Cove.

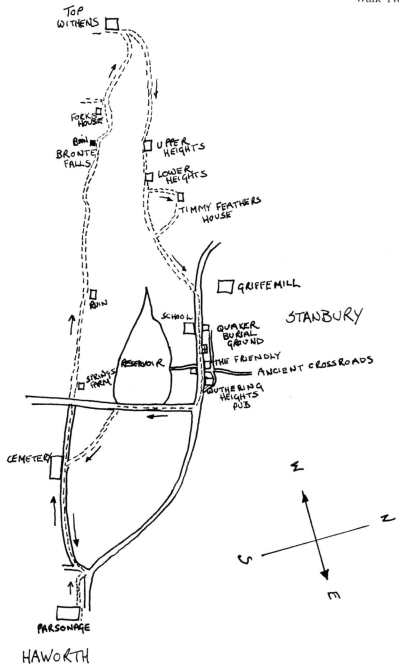

Lily Cove 1886-1906

Lily arrived in Haworth as the star attraction of the 1906 Gala. Her broken body and the mystery surrounding her death forever remain in this hillside grave overlooking the flight path of her last tragic balloon ascent.

Born in the East End of London in 1886, Lily was brought up by her father, a shoemaker called Charles Thomas Cove. The whereabouts of Lily's mother are not known, a fact which only adds to the mystery. It was a time of great social change: the massed rallies and protests that accompanied the emergence of the Suffragette movement would have had a profound effect on the nation and would have certainly influenced young Lily, living in the midst of it all.

Young, vivacious and attractive, she took up employment in the balloon factory of Captain Bidmead. These daring flyers would ascend by balloon to a predetermined height perched upon a

trapeze. A thin cord attached their parachutes to the balloon mesh and when the aeronaut jumped the cord would break, leaving them to parachute safely to the ground. This was extremely hazardous and accidents were common, but this fact seems to have excited rather than deterred Lily, and it wasn't long before she was flying herself, initially jumping in tandem in a dual harness with Captain Bidmead, then going solo. By the time she arrived in Haworth, although only twenty years of age, she had already made twenty successful balloon ascents at various fetes and galas around the country, epitomizing as she went everything the Women's Liberation Movement stood for.

Saturday 11 June 1906

On the day of the Gala thousands of people turned up from neighbouring towns and villages to watch the spectacle. They were to be disappointed. It was a hot, humid day and the balloon failed to rise in the still air. After six attempts the event was called off. Albert Booth, the secretary of the Gala Committee, believed the omens to be bad and tried to dissuade Lily from rescheduling the event to a later date. Lily would not hear of it and insisted that she would try again on the Monday evening.

On Monday the crowds once more turned out to the gala field (now the cricket pitch on West Lane). This time the balloon ascended without incident and Lily flew high over the valley waving at the crowds below. Ten minutes later she was dead, her broken, twisted body lying in a field at the side of Ponden Reservoir, detached from her parachute. How she became separated from her parachute is just one of the mysteries surrounding her death. Suspended beneath it as she was, only she herself could have unhooked it. As a non-swimmer, did she believe she was going to land in the water, and so unhooked herself so as not to become entangled, or was there a more sinister reason? Captain Bidmead himself had inspected her harness prior to the ascent and the inquest found no evidence of foul play. As a liberated woman she is likely to have encountered jealousy and disdain in some quarters. Outspoken, lively and undoubtedly brave, not everyone approved of the way she 'flaunted' herself, showing her legs to all and sundry, and travelling around the country with a man who was not her husband. What really happened that day we shall never know.

When Charles Merrall, son of a local mill owner, who had followed Lily's flight in his motor car, brought news of her death back to Haworth, shock and a great feeling of sadness descended on the village. Her body was brought back in a covered cart and she was laid out in the Old White Lion. Talk about the beginnings of a romance between Lily and Charles Merrall were rife, but unfounded. The inquest could find no answers and a verdict of accidental death was recorded. If her life was something of an enigma so was her death, and perhaps that is how it should be. Lily's tombstone was erected by public subscription.

Turning left, take the path around the edge of the cemetery following it around. Just past the path cutting off to the right, set back, is the grave of Oliver Preston.

Oliver Preston

Oliver Preston was a money lender in Keighley. On the eve of the Keighley feast he was visited by Fred Gill, a local man who wished to borrow money to take his girlfriend away to Whitehaven for the weekend. The following

27

morning Oliver Preston was found dead, his head caved in by an iron bar which had been left at the scene. The police traced the murder weapon to a local foundry where Fred Gill worked. He was subsequently found guilty of the murder and was hanged the following year.

Coming out through the cemetery gates take the route to the left and follow the road towards the reservoir. Cross over the road and onto the farm track.

The Moors

Definition: An area usually unenclosed, of high uncultivated ground with low shrubs.

Man's clearing of the forest which covered the area coupled with climatic changes have left us with the landscape we see today - a landscape so vividly portrayed in Emily Brontë's *Wuthering Heights*. As the forest declined trees were replaced by the grasses and heather. The climate became colder and only the hardiest of plants could survive on the exposed hillsides. Peat, the semi-decomposed remains of plants, unable to turn into topsoil due to lack of oxygen, acts like a sponge soaking up the rainfall before releasing it into the fast flowing streams. The peat bogs are notoriously dangerous: the farmer at Intake Farm above the reservoir set out one day for Halifax with his 'piece' goods. His son set out to follow him but never arrived and was never seen or heard of again. The bogs are also said to conceal the body of a murder victim from Drop Farm and a horse and cart.

The moor is now empty save for the ruined dwellings and enclosures where families once lived and worked. Although there may be fairer places with sights and sounds more pleasing to the senses, the beauty of our moor truly lies in the silence and emptiness and the feeling one gets of being a part of something much bigger.

As you pass the ruin of Springs Farm (built circa 1761), looking over the water towards the village of Stanbury, you can see the cart track known as Waterhead Lane. From ancient times Stanbury stood at a crossroads: its routes travelling north to the Lake District, west to Lancashire, east to Leeds and

Pontefract and south down Waterhead Lane to the wool markets at Halifax. The flooding of the valley for the reservoir not only took out the ancient pack horse trail, it also covered a farm and a small mill known as Little Mill (Hazel Mill in the novels of local author Halliwell Sutcliffe).

Continue along the track for approximately 1¼ miles until you reach the Brontë Waterfall.

The Brontë Waterfall

Referred to by the Brontës as 'the meeting of the waters', this place of peace and tranquillity is enjoyed and appreciated by thousands of visitors every year. Cloudbursts and the occasional eruption of the peat bogs have periodically brought huge torrents of water down the beck carrying with them the large boulders which litter the area. One such cloudburst destroyed the old footbridge, a replica of which now stands in its place.

The old Brontë bridge

There were numerous dwellings around the Falls, remnants of which can be found on the hillside facing. The numerous mounds in the fields above the Falls on the Stanbury side are capped remains of the local coal mines. Coal was recorded as being dug here from as early as the fourteenth-century when Robert le Smith was fined 4d for digging coal on the Lord's land. It was a dangerous job: in one of these pits a man called Clayton was buried alive and never found.

With the coming of the age of steam, coal was in demand and shafts were sunk in earnest, running to depths of up to thirty metres. Coal from these mines was used in the local mills, but the seam was thin and difficult to work and the coal was of an inferior quality. With the coming of the railway to Haworth in 1867 cheaper imports of superior quality coal from the large coal fields of the south and east made the local pits economically unviable and they became obsolete.

Cross the bridge, go up the hill and through the kissing gate, following the track to the left in the direction of Top Withens.

Many of the large boulders strewn about the hillside are Ice Age erratics, carried down by the ice sheet, sometimes great distances, and deposited as the ice receded. Gouged and pounded, many of these bear the scars of their journey.

Continue along the path in the direction of Top Withens some 500 metres until you come to a ladder stile. The large timbers lying by the path are all that remains of Forks House Farm. Over the stile and a little further on to your left is a cart track, this joins the ancient road south known as Limersgate.

Lime was an essential commodity and was needed in order to cultivate the area's acidic soil. Some of the lime came in the form of erratics brought down by the ice from the Dales and Lake District. These would have been crushed and burnt in the kilns to the north of here and carted down this track. Lime was important and as such Lime Carriers were given the right of way journeying to and from the kilns.

A short distance down the track on the bank of the stream stood Forks House Mill. This small mill, of which nothing now remains, was built approximately two hundred years ago. A letter in the *Keighley News* of 1866 refers to a gold like mineral being discovered which caused much excitement amongst the local population with young men leaving their jobs to go and dig for the precious metal. The Mill was converted to a stamp mill to extract and process the gold. It was all to no avail as the substance turned out to be worthless and the men who had broken their backs working around the clock gathering it were left bitterly disappointed.

Continue along the footpath until it joins the paved section of the Pennine Way just below Top Withens.

Top Withens

('Wuthering Heights')

More isolated now than it was in the past, it is easy to imagine the betrayed Heathcliff, tormented over the loss of Catherine, living here and exacting his terrible revenge through various forms of devilry and skullduggery. Although the house doesn't resemble the Heights in Emily's novel, its situation high on these empty moors, exposed to the bracing wind and driving rain, could easily have been in her mind. Its walls are thick and its windows narrow to counter the elements. Although there does not appear to be an exact date for the building, some of the stonework suggests the early seventeenth-century. Below Top Withens there were two other farms: Middle and Lower Withens.

Middle Withens

In 1723 David Midgley, Lord of the Manor, left in trust Middle Withens Farm with fifty acres of land forever to 'clothe with food and convenient blue clothes and other necessary wearing apparel ten poor children of the township of Haworth'. The money for this was to be taken from the rent and profits of running the farm in perpetuity.

Take the paved path past Middle and Lower Withens en route to Stanbury until you come to a low white building.

Upper Heights Farm

The Old Isolation Hospital

Built in 1761 and used at one time to house the victims of typhoid and diphtheria, the main building itself has altered little over the years, a large dormitory, now demolished, stood in the field adjacent to the house. Although truly isolated, its setting is quite splendid, with spectacular views over the valley towards Ponden Hall (said to be Thrushcross Grange in *Wuthering Heights*) and the route west to Lancashire.

Come down the track past Lower Heights Farm and take the stile to your left signed the Pennine Way to Buckley Green.

In the nearest cottage lived 'owd Timmy Feather', the Stanbury handloom weaver who forsook the hurried life of the factory and continued to spin and weave his own wares, requiring only the basic sustenance of life until his death in 1910. By this time his unassuming manner and unaffected lifestyle had made him a reluctant celebrity.

Continue through the hamlet in an easterly direction, turning left and down the hill into Stanbury.

Stanbury

Believed to have been a look-out post in Roman times, this strategically placed village is possessed of a history which pre-dates our documented records. As with Haworth it isn't until the Domesday survey, circa 1086, that we begin to learn of its existence. Its Anglo Saxon name probably means stone fort or enclosure, though the Norse stang or meeting point is also a possibility. One rather fanciful theory relates to Oliver Cromwell, who upon pausing with his army here on the way to lay siege to Bradford, inquired of a local as to the name of the village, and receiving the reply Bury, replied "then I stand-Bury", fanciful since Stanbury by name is mentioned in the village survey of 1322, by which time it was already a well established community. It is also difficult to imagine a man of Cromwell's drive and determination not knowing where he was going. But the story has passed into folklore.

Cross the grass verge on the opposite side of the road. In the valley below lie the skeletal remains of Griffe Mill.

Griffe Mill

Griffe Mill was originally built as a cotton spinning mill at the turn of the nineteenth-century. The reason it still stands is due to its inaccessibility, making the removal of its stone an arduous and costly affair. The two cart routes to the mill, the partially tree-lined route north to Oldfield and the steep walled track to Stanbury, would have been difficult to negotiate on the best of days.

The triangle of reeds in front of the building is the mill dam. From this a canal was cut running to the stream. A sluice was used to control the volume of water going into the dam. On the other (right) side of the dam was another sluice and a chute to the water wheel itself. This way the flow of water could be regulated keeping the wheel, and in turn the spinning machines, operating at a constant speed. Steam power was later introduced along with gas lighting, and a weaving shed added, however, its inaccessibility was always a problem and the mill changed hands many times before being finally shut down in 1928.

Walking through the village you will come to a small patch of land opposite the school. This area of grassland was the burial ground of the Stanbury Quakers.

The Quakers

In the turbulent times of the English Civil War (1642-1649), when the Country was once again afflicted with political and religious turmoil, George Fox formed Quakerism. The Quakers' disdain of the 'high church' in favour of a simpler more accessible form of worship brought them into direct conflict with the established order. Not only were Quakers regularly imprisoned, fined and persecuted by the authorities, they were also mistrusted and frowned upon by the public in general. One sickening report tells of a 'friend' being set upon by an angry mob and beaten senseless whilst he was in the process of burying his child.

Although there are no markers, a stone cross fixed into the wall states that forty-five people were buried here. In the house to the left of the graveyard it is possible to make out  the upstairs meeting room used by the Quakers, the doorway now walled up. At the back of the cemetery are the old school house and the blacksmith's.

An old road through the village runs along the back of the main street joining the northern road at the back of the Wuthering Heights public house (formerly known as The Cross). However, we shall continue a short distance along the main street to the small church.

The Church itself is rather severe, being functional rather than decorative. The pulpit is part of the three-decker pulpit used in Haworth Old Church.

A little further along the street we come to the park and The Friendly public house. Opposite The Friendly stood another pub called The Wagon and Horses, the track down the side being the southern prong of the cross we saw earlier from the opposite side of the reservoir.

Being situated at a crossroads had its disadvantages: the Black Death, the fourteenth-century bubonic plague which ravaged Europe, killing a third of its population, killed nearly half the residents of Stanbury.

Walk out of the village passing the old Manor House on the left and continue down the road, taking the road to your right over the reservoir dam (completed in 1925). On crossing the dam take the track to the left, passing the water cache known as the 'blue lagoon', and continue up the hill. The water treatment plant on the left, which is aesthetically pleasing as far as treatment plants go, is known locally as 'Stanbury Cathedral'. At the top of the track turn left taking the road back into Haworth.

The Brontës
of Haworth

By Ann Dinsdale

In 1820 the Reverend Patrick Brontë was appointed Perpetual Curate of Haworth and arrived in the township with his wife Maria and their six children. Haworth remained the family's home for the rest of their lives and Patrick's appointment marked the final stage of his remarkable career.

Patrick Brontë, the first of ten children, was born at Emdale in Northern Ireland on 17 March 1777. His ability and ambition earned him a place at St. John's College, Cambridge, where his family name of Brunty was dropped in favour of the more impressive sounding 'Brontë'. A college education enabled Patrick to leave his humble origins far behind. He was ordained into the Church of England, and by the time he arrived at Haworth he had already held several curacies and was also a published author of both prose and poetry.

The family's life in Haworth did not get off to a good start: Mrs Brontë died of cancer on 15 September 1821, leaving her children to be cared for by her unmarried sister, Elizabeth Branwell. In 1824 the four eldest daughters were sent to the Clergy Daughters' School at Cowan Bridge, near Kirkby Lonsdale (the infamous Lowood School in Charlotte's *Jane Eyre*). In May 1825 Maria was sent home ill from school and died at the Parsonage aged eleven. Ten-year-old Elizabeth also returned home shortly after, only to die on 15 June. In the space of four years the children had lost not only their mother, but also their much-loved older sisters. For the next six years the surviving children remained at the Parsonage together, creating a rich imaginary world chronicled in tiny illustrated books

In 1831 Charlotte was sent to Miss Wooler's school at Roe Head, Mirfield, where she met her lifelong friends, Ellen Nussey and Mary Taylor. Later she became a teacher at Roe Head, taking first Emily then Anne as pupils.

*Emily Brontë's diary paper, 26 June 1837,
showing herself and Anne seated at the dining
room table.*

*The Brontë gun group, painted by
Branwell Brontë*

Portrait of Charlotte Brontë, circa 1850's

With no independent income, it was clear from the start that all the Brontë children would one day have to earn their own living. The only socially acceptable career option open to impoverished middle-class women was teaching, either in a select school or as governess in a private household. Branwell was not faced with the same career restrictions and hoped to become an artist, but his plan to apply to the Royal Academy of Arts in London came to nothing, and a brief attempt to earn a living as a portrait painter in Bradford brought him nothing but debt.

After a brief period as teacher at Miss Patchett's School at Law Hill, near Halifax, Emily was also back at Haworth. Anne survived in the outside world longest, and her second post as governess to the Robinson family at Thorp Green Hall, near York, lasted for five years. Branwell's attempts to earn a living by tutoring and working on the railways ended ignominiously, and he eventually joined Anne at Thorp Green, as tutor to the Robinson's only son. Anne left her employment rather suddenly in June 1845, followed shortly after by Branwell, dismissed in disgrace for 'proceedings bad beyond expression' - allegedly a love affair with his employer's wife.

To escape the dreary life of a governess, the sisters decided to open a school of their own. In order to acquire the necessary language skills Charlotte and Emily spent a year studying in Brussels. On aunt Branwell's death in 1842 they returned to Haworth, and while Emily remained as housekeeper, Charlotte returned to Brussels. By 1845 the family were together again at Haworth, Charlotte suffering the pain of unrequited love for her teacher, Monsieur Heger. The school project foundered - a prospectus was printed but pupils could not be found.

The sisters had continued to write, and in 1846 they used part of aunt Branwell's legacy to finance the publication of a collection of their poems. *Poems* appeared under the pseudonyms of Currer, Ellis and Acton Bell, but despite some favourable reviews only two copies of the book were sold. Charlotte remained undeterred:

> *'Ill success failed to crush us: the mere effort to succeed had given a wonderful zest to existence: it must be pursued. We each set to work on a prose tale: Ellis Bell produced Wuthering Heights, Acton Bell Agnes Grey, and Currer Bell also wrote a narrative in one volume.'*
>
> Charlotte Brontë
> Biographical Notice of Ellis and Acton Bell, 1850

Charlotte's narrative was *The Professor*, already rejected by several publishers when it arrived in July 1847 at the Cornhill office of Smith, Elder and Co. They also rejected *The Professor* (it was published posthumously in 1857), but wrote encouragingly to Charlotte that a new work '*would meet with careful attention*'. Charlotte was already at work on a new novel, *Jane Eyre*, which was speedily accepted and published to instant acclaim in October 1847. Two months later Emily's *Wuthering Heights* and Anne's *Agnes Grey* were published as a three-volume set by Thomas Cautley Newby. Anne's second novel *The Tenant of Wildfell Hall* followed in June 1848.

Branwell was excluded from the secret of his sisters' success. He had been ailing all summer, his health undermined by alcohol and opium addiction. He died suddenly on 24 September 1848 aged thirty-one. It is said that Emily never left the house again after Branwell's funeral. She died from tuberculosis aged thirty on 19 December 1848. Anne was also ill, and although she followed the medical advice available, there was little that anyone could have done to save her. On 24 May she set out for Scarborough to try a sea cure, accompanied by Charlotte and Ellen Nussey. Just four days later, on 28 May 1849, she also died from tuberculosis, aged twenty-nine.

'A Parody', Branwell Brontë's last surviving drawing showing himself being summoned from sleep by death.

Charlotte, fraught with grief, turned to her writing to sustain her. Over the next few years she published two more novels: *Shirley* in 1849 and *Villette* in 1853. She visited London several times, saw the Great Exhibition and met some of the great writers of her day. Charlotte at last found unexpected happiness when she married her father's curate, Arthur Bell Nicholls, on 29 June 1854. The happiness turned out to be short lived: Charlotte died on 31 March 1855, in the early stages of pregnancy, just three weeks before her thirty-ninth birthday. Patrick Brontë lived on at the Parsonage, cared for by his son-in-law, and died there on 7 June 1861, at the age of eighty-four.

Walk Three

Parsonage, Church and Village

Distance: approximately ³/₄ mile

Haworth Parsonage

By Ann Dinsdale

Haworth Parsonage, the home of the Brontë family, was built in 1778-9 using the local millstone grit. The first occupant was the Reverend John Richardson and following his death in 1791 the Parsonage became the home of James Charnock. Little is known about Charnock's twenty-eight years residency at the Parsonage and we are not even certain that he actually occupied the house for all of the period of his incumbency.[1]

In 1820, following Patrick Brontë's appointment as Perpetual Curate, the Parsonage became the home of the Brontë family. The house came rent-free with Patrick's new position, and was to be the family's home for the rest of their lives. The fact that Patrick

[1] For more information see Kellett, Jocelyn, Haworth Parsonage: The home of the Brontës, The Brontë Society, 1977, pp. 17.

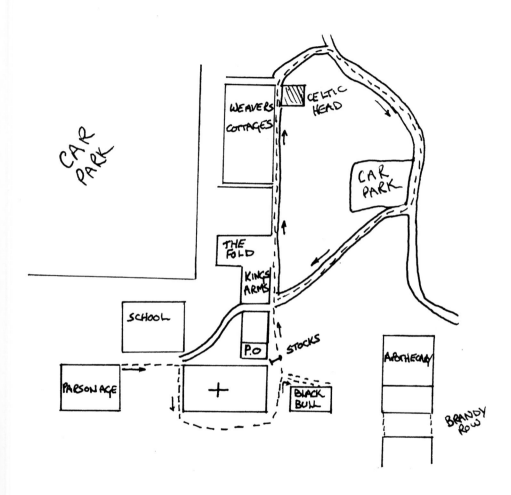

Brontë had no independent income was a source of anxiety for the family, for if his health failed, they stood to lose both income and home. In the event, Patrick Brontë outlived all his family.

The earliest known image of Haworth Parsonage, from an ambrotype photograph dating from the mid-1850s.

After Mr Brontë's death on 7 June 1861, the Parsonage became the home of his successor, the Reverend John Wade. Wade evidently found the Parsonage cramped and inconvenient, and in 1878 outraged many Brontë enthusiasts when he added a large gabled wing to the house, to create more space for his growing family. Other alterations were made to the Brontë part of the house and a visitor at this time remarked how:

Mr Brontë disliked to have mechanical work going on there. Only once, from absolute necessity, to keep out bad leakage, he allowed the roof to be mended. The new incumbent does not choose to go into a rotten old house, but they are doing very much more than making merely necessary repairs. They are putting in fireplaces and mantelpieces of marble, and windows of plate glass, a single pane filling the whole sash and weighing thirty pounds.[2]

Following on from Wade, the Parsonage served as home to three more incumbents: T.W. Storey (1898-1919); G.A. Elson (1919-1925) and J.C. Hirst (1925-1928). In 1928, Sir James Roberts, a local man who had made a fortune in the textile industry, bought the Parsonage for the Brontë Society (founded in 1893) and provided the money to set it up as a museum. In the Museum's early days the Wade wing was adapted to serve as a research library and to provide living accommodation for the resident custodian. In the late 1950s a further extension was added to the rear of the building to create more exhibition space.

[2] Lemon, Charles, ed., *Early Visitors to Haworth: From Ellen Nussey to Virginia Woolf*, The Brontë Society, 1996, pp. 81.

On 4 August 1928 thousands turned out to see the opening of the Brontë Parsonage Museum.

Nowadays the majority of the rooms in the original Brontë part of the house are set out in as close an approximation as possible to their appearance in the Brontës' day, and most of the furniture and objects on display actually belonged to the family. Despite the addition of the Wade wing, and the trees which now soften the bleak graveyard outlook, the Georgian Parsonage still remains very much as the Brontës would have known it.

Walk down the cobbled lane passing the old national schoolhouse on the left, the plaque on the wall reminding us that Charlotte Brontë taught there, and continue down to Haworth Church.

Haworth old church

Haworth Church

Probably built on the site of an Anglo-Saxon field kirk, the church has undergone considerable alterations throughout its history including a number of complete re-builds most notably in 1879 when the Reverend Wade, Patrick Brontë's successor, to the dismay of many, demolished the old church with the exception of the tower, erecting in its place the building we have today. The main reason given for its demolition was the deteriorating state of the interior graves along with the rising level of the ground in the churchyard itself. The practice of placing the deceased 'stacked' in family vaults had over time, resulted in the earth on the outer side of the church wall rising three feet above the church floor. Reports of a black liquid seeping through the walls and forming stagnant puddles were enough to persuade the relevant authorities of a re-build, the condition being that the Brontë family vault within the church itself remained undisturbed.

The vault itself lies to the right of the altar marked by a brass plaque to the memory of Charlotte and Emily. Inscribed into the pillar to the right are the names of all the family members interred here.

In the glass case to the right are a number of articles of interest including Charlotte's marriage certificate along with the seventeenth century bible from Patrick Brontë's study. The memorial tablet inside the Brontë chapel was made by Patrick Brontë's sexton, John Brown, a good friend of Branwell's. Another plaque within the church is a memorial to Patrick Brontë's curate, William Weightman, a man much admired by the family and possibly beloved by Anne. He died tragically of cholera and is buried close by where the pulpit now stands. It has been said that Anne wrote the following moving lines to him:

> *"Yes, though art gone and never more*
> *thy sunny smile shall gladden me;*
> *But I may pass the old church door,*
> *And pace the floor that covers thee,*

May stand upon the cold, damp stone,
And think that frozen, lies below
The lightest heart that I have known,
The kindest I shall ever know."

And later:

"Cold in the grave for years has lain
The form it was my bliss to see;
And only dreams can bring again,
The darling of my heart to me."

Come out of the church and into the churchyard itself. In the church tower, facing the parsonage are a number of small indentations, a result of Patrick Brontë discharging his pistols from his front door.

The Luddites

High unemployment in the wake of the industrial revolution created immeasurable hardships and in turn social unrest. The Luddites and Frame-breakers, formed out of misery and desperation, attempted to halt the great push towards urbanisation and industrialisation by targeting the factories housing the new machines.

Patrick Brontë's outspoken views on the ensuing lawlessness caused him to fear for his own safety, as a consequence he began carrying with him two loaded pistols, which he would then discharge for safety reasons every morning

Walking around the tower the sundial on the south facing side was donated by Richard Pollard of Stanbury, his grave lying at the base. A generous man , he made provision in his will that fifty shillings from his estate be donated annually to the poor of Haworth and Stanbury.

Haworth Churchyard

By Ann Dinsdale

One of the striking features of the Brontës' parsonage home is the melancholy churchyard, crammed full of graves, which surrounds the house on two sides. The Brontës themselves were buried in a family vault beneath the church floor (with the exception of Anne who died at Scarborough and was laid to rest in St Mary's Churchyard). Buried outside in the churchyard are many of the family's neighbours, friends and servants.

Although the burial registers for the churchyard go back to 1645, some of the gravestones pre-date this. It is claimed that 40,000 people are buried here, and a wander round the churchyard can tell you a lot about their lives. Gravestones often indicate a person's interests or occupation (look out for the graves of musicians decorated with musical scores or those of stonemasons showing the tools of their trade). They also indicate what an appallingly unhealthy place Haworth was in which to live.

In 1849 Patrick Brontë organized petitions to
the General Board of Health which resulted in
Benjamin Herschel Babbage spending three
days in Haworth to conduct an investigation
into the township's sanitary arrangements.
Babbage's report (published in 1850) paints a
grim picture of a village littered with stagnant
pools and refuse heaps. The only sewerage
system consisted of open channels running
down the Main Street and a dozen families
might share a single privy. All these hazards
to public health were exacerbated by the poor
water supply, which was inadequate for the
needs of the population and also heavily
contaminated by deadly seepage from the
graveyard, situated above the level of most of
the public wells and pumps. One of these wells
supplied water to around 150 households, but
often during the summer months the supply
was said to turn so green and putrid that cattle
would refuse to drink the water it provided.

Haworth churchyard was ill-drained and
overcrowded, posing a constant threat to the
health of the living. Babbage was extremely
concerned by the practice of covering graves
with large flat stones which prevented the
growth of plants and shrubs which would
assist decomposition. The trees we see in the
graveyard today were planted in the 1860s as

a result of Babbage's report. He noted that there had been 1,344 burials in the previous ten years alone, and recommended that the graveyard be closed immediately. It wasn't until late in the nineteenth century however, that a new cemetery was opened on the edge of the moors.

Large families lived in cramped, squalid conditions, often living and sleeping in one room. Infectious diseases spread very quickly. Many of the graves are those of young children, and in fact in the mid-nineteenth century forty-one per cent of the children born in Haworth died before reaching the age of six. One grave contains the seventeen children of Joseph and Frances Leeming. One of the most striking gravestones is that of James Whitham Heaton who died aged one and was buried with his five little brothers and sisters. The gravestone was lovingly carved by the children's father and decorated with the stone figure of a sleeping child, said to resemble James. The baby's arms are often filled with wild flowers, placed there by visitors who are moved by the sad story.

Though the Brontë deaths were tragically premature, they were certainly not remarkable in a village where the average life expectancy was twenty-five years, corresponding with that of some of the most unhealthy districts of London. A wander around Haworth churchyard reminds us that although the Brontës suffered, they did not suffer alone.

Taking the path around the church towards the wrought iron gates, a grave by the tree at the side of the Black Bull contains one of the churchyard's more notorious residents. The stone simply reads JS 1796 and is the last resting place of James Sutcliffe, a highwayman, who was convicted and hanged at York, his body then being brought back and laid to rest here.

Come out through the gates and onto the main street, to the right is the famous Black Bull Inn.

The Black Bull

Built in the eighteenth century from millstone grit the Inn became a regular haunt for Branwell and his companions. A lively character and a brilliant conversationalist, he would often be sent for when an unaccompanied traveller arrived at the pub in need of companionship.

A replica of his chair, along with the bell-pull used to summon more drinks, can be found inside.

Brandy Row

The archway across the street connecting what is now Emma's Cafe and the ice cream parlour led into a rabbit warren of terraces known as Brandy Row, the name originating from the wine and spirit merchants who were situated there.

The area, which housed 142 persons, many of them engaged in woolcombing was severely criticised in the 1851 Health Report, for the diseases and filthiness found therein.

The Druggist Store, still known as the Apothecary, was where Branwell purchased his opium.

The Stocks

At the side of the church steps are the village 'stocks'. Prior to the rebuilding of the church, the stocks were directly in front of the church gates at the side of the Black Bull. In a less tolerant age offenders would be placed in these for the purpose of public humiliation.

The gift shop by the stocks was at one time the village post office, from where the Brontës dispatched their handwritten manuscripts to their respective publishers.

The Kings Arms

Initially the property of the Lord of the Manor of Haworth, the Manorial Courts were held here in an upstairs room, up until the end of the 19th century. At the rear of the pub is a small courtyard called The Fold, (note the old privies in the far right corner). A stand-pipe from which the villagers would draw water also stood here, though its close proximity to the churchyard would have made its supply particularly hazardous.

Continue along West Lane passing the row of weaver's and woolcomber's cottages on your left. The rows of windows allowing as much light as possible into the workshops, essential in the time prior to the introduction of gas lighting.

Continue to the end of the street pausing for a moment by the end house on the right opposite the car park. Fixed into the corner of the building is a celtic head.

Celtic Heads

The Celts came to these islands from central Europe around 500 BC. They believed the head to be the vehicle of the soul, and would often retain the heads of slain enemies, believing that in doing so they acquired something of their victim's strength and spirit.

Prior to the advent of mass communication, superstition and folklore would often become intertwined with fact, the three lying inseparable in the subconsciousness of the relevant populace.

Although pre-christian in origin, of the 200 effigies of heads found around the area not all are ancient, and it can be assumed that the cult of revering the head possibly for luck or fertility continued in more isolated areas, albeit in a low profile, up to as recently as the eighteenth century.

Turning right at the junction walk down the pavement passing the seventeenth century farm house on the left, turn right up North Street and a short distance past the Police Station is one of the village's oldest houses. The date stone above the door bearing the inscription 1671. The road will bring you back to Main Street.

Walk Four

Besides the Brontës ...
By Robert Swindells

Distance: approximately 500 metres

Ask anyone on Haworth Main Street which
famous persons are commemorated in the
village and they'll say the Bronte sisters;
Charlotte, Emily and Anne. A few might
include their brother Branwell and the
Reverend Patrick. Nobody will mention Tom
Mix or Amy Johnson, yet commemorative
slabs to both of these celebrities are to be seen
in the village.

No, they are not in the churchyard, but if you
follow the footpath which links the church
yard with the Bronte Village car park you'll
step on Tom Mix's slab about halfway along.
It's got his picture on it, wearing a ten-gallon
hat, and the name's engraved underneath. It's
not the finest example you'll ever see of the

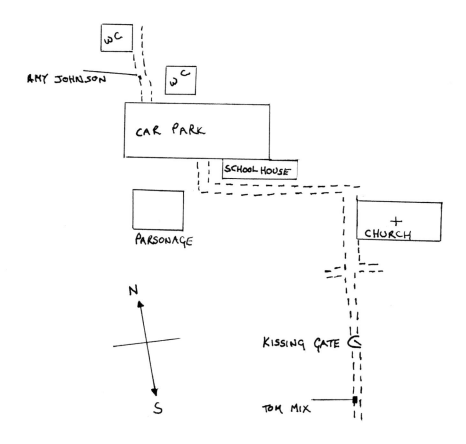

stonemason's craft, but it's a fair bet the tribute came straight from the heart of the youngster who took the trouble painstakingly to carve it, almost certainly sometime in the thirties.

So who *was* Tom Mix? He was one of the earliest film cowboys, back in the silent days. His first picture, shot in 1910, was called *Ranch Life in the Great Southwest.* As a title it doesn't trip off the tongue, but Tom went on to star in literally scores of western movies and to become an idol to countless youngsters on both sides of the Atlantic. When the advent of talkies put paid to his screen career (his voice lacked necessary gravel) he formed and performed in his own wild west circus, which he named the Tom Mix Circus. Okay so titles weren't his strong suit, but if there'd been no Tom Mix there'd probably have been no James Stewart or John Wayne or Clint Eastwood either. Tom died in a car crash in 1940.

And Amy Johnson? Amy was a pioneer pilot and the first female aero engineer in the world. Born in Hull, she learned to fly in 1929. In 1930 she flew a flimsy, single engined biplane 11,000 miles from England to Australia, becoming the first woman ever to make such a flight alone.

*The Tom Mix
Flagstone*

Robert Swindells

The Amy Johnson flagstone

Robert Swindells

Over the next few years she clocked up a number of other record-breaking flights, including one to Japan and two to Cape Town, becoming an idol in Britain and a celebrity whose name was a household word around the globe. Songs were composed in her honour. Proposals of marriage arrived daily in the post. Crowds lined the streets to cheer her wherever she went. A pop-record, *Amy, Wonderful Amy* was a much requested favourite on BBC radio. In a Yorkshire village, a child chipped the likeness of a small plane and the name Amy Johnson on a flagstone. To view this, start outside the gents' convenience adjacent to the Museum car park and walk up towards the car park, scrutinising the slabs near the wall on your right. Amy's stone is approximately opposite the entrance to the ladies' convenience.

Amy Johnson was killed in 1941 when a plane she was flying as a member of the wartime Air Transport Auxiliary went down in the Thames Estuary. She was 38.

The stone was etched in the 1930s at Rock Street, in Keighley by a boy named Eric Sawley using a hammer and nail.
When Rock Street was demolished the flagstones were reused at Haworth.